HOW TO SPEAK BASEBALL

HOW *to* SPEAK

Baseball

JAMES CHARLTON

SALLY COOK

ILLUSTRATIONS *by* ROSS MᶜDONALD

AN ILLUSTRATED GUIDE TO BALLPARK BANTER

CHRONICLE BOOKS
SAN FRANCISCO

Library of Congress Cataloging-in-Publication Data is
available.

ISBN: 978-1-4521-2645-6

Manufactured in China

Designed by Neil Egan
Additional Typesetting by DC Type

10 9 8 7 6 5 4

Chronicle Books LLC
680 Second Street
San Francisco, California 94107
www.chroniclebooks.com

To Four Special Daniels

. . . .

To Jame-boy

Introduction

Baseball is the oldest of America's team sports, and probably the richest in colorful vocabulary. One dictionary lists more than 5,000 terms used in the game, and those are constantly being added to—by players, coaches, fans, and commentators.

Some of the new additions to the lexicon are from Hall of Fame pitcher turned announcer, Dennis Eckersley, who describes how to pitch: "Pitching is simple—cheese for the kitchen [inside pitch] and a yakker [curveball] for the kudo [the little bow a batter takes when he bails out on a curve]." If that description doesn't make you dizzy, you'll probably dig another Eckersley observation: "The manager has had enough of this salad. He's going to the bullpen to find someone who can really bring the cheese. He's looking for someone to bring the gas, a little high cheddar with some hair on it, maybe to buzz this dude's moss and set it up so he can paint for a punch out." Got it?

You'll find that many of the terms have become common in our everyday English. To name a few: southpaw, bush league, fastball, down the middle, hit it out of the park, it's the bottom of the ninth, threw me a curve, closer, and bullpen.

The use of baseball images abounds in daily life: The word strike is pervasive in common English. When a person has failed we say they've "struck out." Or how about this one? "He stepped up to the plate" refers to a person who takes on his responsibilities.

We've mined a bountiful source in bringing you this compendium of baseball slang, popular and obscure, new and old. We think the stories and illustrations that accompany these terms are as much fun as the rich lexicon. We hope you'll agree.

AIRMAIL

Ace: A team's best pitcher.

. . . .

Airmail: A throw over another player's head that is too high to catch. No postage necessary.

. . . .

Alley: The section of the field between outfielders. A hit in the alley between the center fielder and either the right or left fielder usually goes for extra bases.

APPLE

Apple: A baseball. Made of horsehide up until 1974, when a switch was made to cowhide, presumably making horses happy.

. . . .

Around the horn: Throwing the ball around the infield during practice or after an out is made. An around-the-horn double play goes from third to second to first. The origins of the phrase are generally ascribed to sailing around Cape Horn.

Aspirin: A pitch thrown so hard it looks as small as an aspirin or a pill to the batter. This one *gives* you a headache.

. . . .

Backdoor curve: A pitch thrown to a hitter by a pitcher of opposite handedness that starts outside the plate, then curves sharply in over the back half of the plate, and is called a strike. A **slider**. Manager Charlie Dressen once called it "the worst pitch in baseball. It slides over the plate and then out of the ballpark."

. . . .

Backward K: In scorekeeping, a K indicates a swinging third strike. A backward K signifies a third strike called by the umpire.

. . . .

Bag: A base. A **two-bagger** is a double, and a **three-bagger** is a triple. The three bases are made of soft material covered by canvas, hence the term "bag." Home plate is flat and made of hard rubber, not really a bag, but a home run is a **four-bagger**. Go figure!

BACKDOOR CURVE

BALL HAWK

BALL HAS EYES

Ball has eyes: When the ball appears to see the gloves and elude them. What if the gloves have eyes?

. . . .

Ball hawk: A speedy outfielder who can run down long line drives.

. . . .

Baltimore chop: A batted ball that takes a high bounce after hitting the ground in front of home plate. By the time the ball comes down, the batter has reached first base. Named after the tactic used by several hitters, including the legendary John McGraw at the turn of the last century, who took advantage of the sun-baked ground in front of Baltimore's home plate.

· · · · · · · · · · · · · ·

Bandbox: A small ballpark. No Major League stadiums today would be called bandboxes. Baker Bowl, home of the Philadelphia Phillies, qualified as the Major League's premier bandbox in 1923. The left field fence was 335 feet from home plate, and center field was a respectable 408 feet. But the right field fence was a cozy 272 feet away, making it an inviting target for left-handed hitters.

· · · · · · · · · · · · · ·

Bang-bang play: The almost simultaneous arrival of the ball in the fielder's glove and the runner at the base.

· · · · · · · · · · · · · ·

Banjo hitter: A hitter with no power. He hits the ball like he is using a banjo, not a bat.

BANJO
HITTER

BASKET CATCH

EXTRA INNINGS: Banjo hitter

Duane Kuiper, a banjo hitter with a career batting average of .271, went to bat 3,379 times, hitting only one home run, while playing for the Cleveland Indians. When the Indians traded him to the Giants in 1981, they gave him the seat where his home run landed.

Barnburner: An exciting, high-scoring game in which the lead goes back and forth.

. . . .

Barnstorming: Playing exhibition games in small towns or cities. Teams used to barnstorm north after spring training was over and before the season opened. After the season, many players would barnstorm to make extra money.

. . . .

Basket catch: Catching a fly ball with the palm of the glove up and at waist height. The signature catch of Willie Mays.

Battery: The catcher and pitcher together. Alone, each is called a **battery mate**. The term was first used in the 1860s. While there are several theories about the origin, the most popular has to do with a military "battery" or gun.

. . . .

Bazooka: The arm of a fast pitcher. A **flame-thrower** is a pitcher with a bazooka (also, gun or cannon) for an arm. A position player, too, can have a gun for an arm. Carl Furillo, a Dodger right fielder from Reading, Pennsylvania, was nicknamed "The Reading Rifle" because of his strong throwing arm.

. . . .

BB: A pitch thrown so hard it looks like a BB. Conversely, when a batter is hitting the ball well, the ball appears as big as a grapefruit.

. . . .

Beanball: A pitch that is thrown at the batter's head.

BAZOOKA

BELLY WHOPPER

Belly whopper: A runner sliding into base on his stomach. In years past, most players slid feet first but today most base runners try to beat the tag by skidding in on their stomachs.

. . . .

Bench jockey: A player who yells at the opposing team from the dugout.

EXTRA INNINGS: Bench jockey

In a famous incident in Game 3 of the 1932 World Series, the Cubs' bench jockeys were loudly riding the Yankees' Babe Ruth. The game was tied at four runs apiece and Ruth, who already had a homer in the game, had two strikes on him in the fifth. Ruth glared at the rowdy Cubs bench, then gestured toward the outfield. On the next pitch he slammed a homer to center field and ignited a controversy that still continues: did the Babe call his shot as a challenge to the bench jockeys, or did he signal to pitcher Charlie Root that he had one more swing coming?

Bench player: A player not in the starting lineup, available as a substitute.

. . . .

The Bigs: The Major Leagues. Also known as **The Show**.

BIRD DOG

Bingle: A base hit, a single. However, a double is not a bubble.

. . . .

Bird dog: A scout who looks for prospective players. A pooch with an eagle eye.

. . . .

Blazer: A really good fastball. A **bullet**.

. . . .

Bleachers: The uncovered seats without backrests in the outfield, usually the cheapest seats in the house. The regulars who sit there are called **Bleacher Bums**, a colorful collection of fans. They often go shirtless and serenade players. The Bleacher Bums at Wrigley Field started the practice of throwing back home runs by opposing players.

. . . .

Bleeder: A weakly batted ground ball that goes for a hit.

Blooper: A weakly hit fly ball that drops in for a single between an infielder and an outfielder. Also called a **bloop single**. Pirates announcer Bob Prince would say, "What we need now is a bloop and a blast."

. . . .

Blue: Umpires. They have traditionally worn dark blue, although they have been known to appear in light blue, black, or maroon shirts.

BLUE

Blue chipper: A high school or college prospect who is considered a "can't miss" player. Since the amateur players draft started in 1965, number one picks failed only twice to make the majors, and that was because of career-ending injuries.

EXTRA INNINGS: Blue

The Major Leagues now use four umpires in a game, and six during postseason play. Before 1898 only a single umpire was used in a game, leading to all sorts of chicanery. If the lone umpire was looking at a play in the outfield, the base runner might cut directly from first to third, skipping second base. Or the runner might be tripped, grabbed, or elbowed by the fielders as he made his way around the bases. In 1898, two umpires became the rule, which still holds in the low minors. The high minors use three umpires.

Blue darter: A low, hard-hit line drive. The term was first associated with the great hitter Shoeless Joe Jackson, and later made popular by announcer Dizzy Dean.

. . . .

Bonehead play: A really dumb mental mistake.

. . . .

Boot: To make an error, usually on a ground ball. Len Merullo, a Cubs shortstop in the '40s, once made four errors in a game on four consecutive ground balls. His wife gave birth to a daughter the same day, and Merullo's teammates suggested he name the baby "Boots." Wisely, he ignored them.

. . . .

Box: In the early days of baseball, there was no mound or pitching rubber. Rather, pitchers threw from a box drawn on the field, much like a batter's box is drawn on the field today. While pitchers boxes have long been replaced by a pitching rubber, the term still exists. For

BONEHEAD PLAY

instance, a hit back through the middle is called **back through the box**; when a pitcher who has been hit hard is taken out of the game, he is **knocked out of the box**.

. . . .

Bread-and-butter pitch: A pitch that a hurler feels he can rely on to get a batter out. It could get the pitcher out of a jam.

BRUSH BACK

Break your wrists: When a batter starts to swing but holds up in the middle because he doesn't like the pitch or was fooled by it. Whether or not he swung too far and "broke his wrists" determines whether a ball or strike is called. No medical doctor or cast needed.

. . . .

Bring it: When a pitcher throws a hard strike.

. . . .

Bronx cheer: A loud derisive sound made with the tongue sticking out. A **raspberry**. The origin is unknown, but is believed by some to relate to the early, mediocre days of the Yankees.

. . . .

Brushback: An inside pitch that forces the batter to back away from the plate.

. . . .

Bullpen: Where each team's relief pitchers warm up before entering a game.

EXTRA INNINGS: Bullpen

Most bullpens are separate areas behind the outfield, but in venerable Wrigley Field the bullpens are set in foul territory down the right and left field lines. This can occasionally present problems, such as what happened in the eighth inning of a tie game in 1929. Cubs batter Norm McMillan hit a line drive down the left field line with the bases loaded, and Reds outfielder Evar Swanson couldn't find the ball, which he had seen bounce off a gutter in foul territory. McMillan circled the bases for a grand slam. Later, Cubs reliever Ken Penner picked up his jacket on the bullpen bench and the ball dropped out of his right sleeve.

Bush league: Refers to a poorly made play. The Minor Leagues are known as the **bushes**.

. . . .

Buzz the tower: A high, inside pitch thrown by a pitcher to either intimidate the hitter, get

him to stop crowding the plate, or set up the
next pitch thrown on the outside of the plate.

. . . .

Cactus league: Spring training games in
Arizona.

. . . .

Cakewalk: A game where one team wins by a
big score.

CACTUS
LEAGUE

Can of corn: An easy fly ball to catch. Easier to catch than a sack of potatoes.

. . . .

Carpet: Infield surface. The term is also used for artificial turf.

. . . .

Catbird seat: Being in the top or most advantageous position, like a batter with a three ball, no strike count. The term was first used by Red Barber, a Brooklyn Dodgers announcer of the 1940s.

. . . .

Caught looking: A third strike that catches the hitter with his bat on his shoulder.

. . . .

Changeup: A pitch thrown with a fastball motion but comes to the plate much more slowly. An off-speed pitch that looks like a fastball—but the pitcher seemingly pulls a string to slow the ball down.

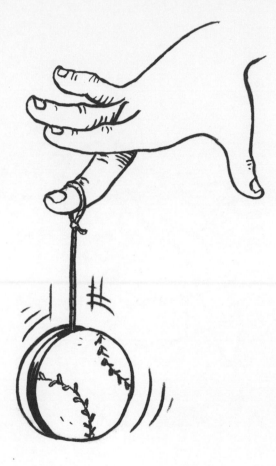

CHANGEUP

CHIN
MUSIC

Checked swing: When the batter starts to swing but holds up. Often the catcher will ask the ump whether it was a checked swing or did the batter commit far enough that it was a strike.

. . . .

Cheese (hard cheese): A hard fastball. Also called **high heat** or **express**. A Gouda pitch.

. . . .

Chin music: An inside pitch close to a batter's chin. (If the ball comes any closer, the batter might be singing a different tune.) A **shave**. A pitcher who throws a lot of chin music is called a **barber**. NY Giants pitcher Sal Maglie was known as "The Barber" because he threw so many high inside pitches.

. . . .

Choke up: When a batter moves his hands up from the knob at the end of the bat. A hitter loses power by choking up, but gains some bat control. Few hitters choke up these days. Wee Willie Keeler, a Hall of Famer who played at the turn of the last century, was known for it. He choked up so far that Sam Crawford, another Hall of Famer, said, "He only used half the bat."

. . . .

Chopper: A batted ball taking several bounces to reach an infielder.

. . . .

Chucker: A pitcher. Also a **hurler**, a **slab man**, a **moundsman**.

. . . .

Cleanup hitter: The batter hitting fourth in the lineup, usually a slugger. He tries to clean the bases of runners.

. . . .

Cliff-hanger: A game where the outcome is decided at the last minute.

. . . .

Climb the ladder: On successive pitches a pitcher throws the ball higher and higher, attempting to entice the batter to swing above

CLIMB the LADDER

the strike zone. **Down the ladder** is throwing pitches progressively lower. Camilo Pascual, an American League pitcher in the '50s and '60s, pitched down the ladder with his great curveball.

· · · · · · · · · · · · · · · · ·

Clothesline: A hard-hit line drive with no arc to it.

COMEBACKER

Clubhouse lawyer: A player who stirs up trouble against the management in the clubhouse.

. . . .

Comebacker: A ground ball hit right back to the pitcher.

. . . .

Cookie: An easy pitch to hit.

. . . .

Cousin: A favorite pitcher for a batter to hit against, or a pitcher's favorite batter. Occasionally, a cousin can refer to a team's performance against a particular pitcher. Herm Wehmeier was 0-14 against the Cardinals and must have breathed a sigh of relief when, after his final loss to St. Louis, he was traded to them.

. . . .

Crackerjack: A fine play or player, and the best snack in the game.

CRANK

Crank: A nineteenth-century term for a fan of a team.

. . . .

Cup of coffee: A Minor League player who makes an appearance or two in the majors.

CUP *of* COFFEE

EXTRA INNINGS: Cup of coffee

Some players barely have a sip of coffee. In 1971, pitcher Larry Yount hurt his arm warming up in his Major League debut and had to be replaced before he ever threw a pitch. He never appeared in another game. His brother, Robin, had more success and is now in the Hall of Fame.

Curtain call: After a great play or game, coming out of the dugout to acknowledge the fans' cheers. The first curtain call in baseball occurred in 1956, when Dale Long set a record by homering in eight straight games. After his eighth homer, the Pittsburgh fans continued to applaud, and Long's teammates pushed him out of the dugout so that he could acknowledge the cheers.

. . . .

Curtain raiser: The first game in a series. Hoping for some good plays!

. . . .

Curveball: A pitched ball that curves because of the spin put on it. Candy Cummings, a nineteenth-century pitcher, is usually given credit for throwing the first curveball. Yankee pitching coach Jim Turner called a good curveball a "Kansas City Kitty," though no one knows why. Also called a **snake**.

CURTAIN CALL

CUTIE

Cutie (cutey): A pitcher who uses curves and off-speed pitches, rather than an overpowering fastball. A **junkball pitcher**.

. . . .

Cycle: When a player hits a single, double, triple, and homer in the same game. A natural cycle would be getting the hits in order. Ty Cobb, Willie Mays, and Babe Ruth are three stars who never hit for a cycle, while Ruth's teammate Bob Meusel did it a record three times.

. . . .

Day at the beach: An easy game. The loser gets burned.

. . . .

Dead red: When a batter gets the pitch that he expects (usually a fastball), he is sitting dead red. This usually occurs on a hitter's count—2-1 or 3-1—when the pitcher needs to get a strike.

DIG IN

Dig in: A batter walks into the batter's box, getting his feet comfortable by moving them around until his spikes settle into the dirt, the same way a golfer might "dig in" before driving a ball off the tee.

Dish: When the pitcher throws. As in: "Here comes the dish." As a pitcher winds up and dishes, it's called **wheeling and dealing**. Dish is also used as a term for home plate.

. . . .

Doctor the ball: Anything that a pitcher can do to a ball that will alter its flight to the plate. This includes scratching, cutting a seam, and adding saliva, talcum powder, or grease to decrease the friction of the fingers on the ball. Pitchers have been caught having Vaseline in their mitts, a file in their pocket, or a belt buckle with a sharp point on it.

DOCTOR the BALL

DOWN UNDER

Down under: Pitching a **submarine ball** (delivering a pitch from the 5 o'clock arm slot). Some pitchers scrape their knuckles on the ground when they throw down under. Pitcher David Cone called his down under pitch a Laredo, after the far south Texas border town. Cone's high pitch, however, was not called a Fargo.

Downtown: A long home run. To **go yard**. Also called a **tater**, a **dinger**, a **four-bagger**, or a **dial 8**, from the term for dialing long distance in a hotel room.

. . . .

Dribbler: A barely hit ground ball. A swinging bunt. Give this batter a bib.

DRIBBLER

DUSTER

Ducks on the pond: Runners on the bases: almost always used when there are three ducks on the pond, or the bases are loaded. Perhaps collisions should be called quack-ups.

. . . .

Duster: An inside fastball that sends the batter sprawling in the dust to avoid being hit. A duster is often thrown in retaliation for the other team's pitcher hitting a batter with a pitch.

. . . .

Dying quail: A softly hit ball that goes just over the infielder's head, and drops in safely before an outfielder can reach it. Also called a **duck snort**.

. . . .

Farm team: A Minor League team of a Major League club. The Major League team owns the players, managers, and coaches, but not the stadium and concessions.

Fastball: The most used pitch in the Major Leagues. An average fastball clocks in on the radar gun at 88 to 90 mph, and a good one at over 90 mph. A few pitchers can hurl a fastball over 100 mph.

. . . .

Fat pitch: An easy pitch to hit. A **lollipop**, a **cookie**, a **meatball**. Put this pitcher on a diet.

. . . .

Fireballer: A fastball pitcher. One of the more interesting fireballers was a relief pitcher named Ryne Duren, who pitched for the Yankees and other teams in the mid-20th century. He was nearly blind and wore Coke-bottle thick glasses. When he was a minor leaguer one scout said, "He throws so hard batters can't see it. But he can't see them either."

. . . .

Fireman: A relief pitcher who comes into the game to put out the fire when the other team threatens to score by putting runners on base.

FAT PITCH

FIFTY-FIVE FOOTER

Fifty-five footer: A derisive term for a pitch. The distance between the pitching rubber and home plate is sixty feet, six inches. Hence, a pitch that goes fifty-five feet bounces before it gets there.

. . . .

Five-tool player: A scouting term referring to a player who has all the skills: hitting, hitting for power, speed on the basepaths, good fielding, good throwing arm. The guy with the power tools.

FLAMETHROWER

Flare: A softly hit line drive over the infield, usually to the opposite field. Also called a **Texas Leaguer**.

. . . .

Flamethrower: A pitcher who throws a good fastball.

. . . .

Flipper: A pitcher's arm. A pitcher's **wing**. His **soupbone**.

Fly chaser: An outfielder. A speedy outfielder is a **ball hawk**.

. . . .

Fog it by: To hurl a fastball past the batter. To throw some **hard cheese**.

. . . .

Foot in the bucket: A batting stance where the hitter's front foot pulls away toward either first or third base, and his back foot stays firm, as if in a water bucket. This stance can be deliberate, or the result of the batter's fear of being hit or fooled by the ball. Al Simmons, a Hall of Famer, is probably the best known for hitting that way. His nickname was "Bucketfoot Al."

. . . .

Forkball: Similar to a split-finger fastball, a ball thrown with a fastball motion but that doesn't travel as rapidly, and drops as it gets close to the plate. The ball is jammed down

FOOT IN the BUCKET

between the pitcher's index and middle fingers.
A difficult pitch to throw and for the batter to
pick up. Roy Face, a reliever for the Pirates in
1959, perfected this pitch and went 18–1 for the
season.

. . . .

Free swinger: A batter who regularly swings at
pitches outside the strike zone. Not what you
probably thought.

GLOVE MAN

Frozen rope: A hard-hit line drive.

. . . .

Glove man: A good fielder. Often refers to a player who made the team because of his glove, not his bat. Batman he's not, yet he's robbin' batters of hits.

. . . .

Go yard: Hitting a homer over the fence.

Golden sombrero: What a batter is said to wear when he strikes out four times in a game. If only the ball were a piñata.

GOLDEN SOMBRERO

Gonfalon: An old-fashioned term for a pennant. The term was famously noted in a poem by Franklin P. Adams, published in the *New York Evening Mail* in 1910.

> *These are the saddest of possible words:*
> *"Tinker to Evers to Chance."*
> *Trio of bear cubs, and fleeter than birds,*
> *Tinker and Evers and Chance.*
> *Ruthlessly pricking our gonfalon bubble,*
> *Making a Giant hit into a double—*
> *Words that are heavy with nothing but trouble:*
> *"Tinker to Evers to Chance."*

. . . .

Goose egg: On the scoreboard, a scoreless inning is a zero, or goose egg. The ducks on the pond don't reach home.

. . . .

Gopher ball: A pitch hit for a home run. The pitcher digs a hole for himself.

GRAND SALAMI

Grand salami: A nickname for a grand slam, a homer with the bases loaded. Dave Neihaus, the announcer for the Mariners, had a signature call whenever a Seattle player hit a grand slam: "Get out the rye bread and mustard, Grandma, it is grand salami time!"

HANDCUFFED

Grapefruit league: Spring training games in Florida.

. . . .

Green light: When the coach signals to the batter that he's got the okay to swing at a pitch, usually in an obvious situation when the batter has no strikes and three balls. A base runner can also get a green light from a coach.

. . . .

Handcuffed: The result of a pitch that overpowers the batter, or a pitch that the batter is not expecting, for instance, a changeup when he is expecting a fastball or a fastball when he is expecting a curve. Also, the result of a hit that an infielder can't handle. An infielder can be handcuffed by a hard-hit ground ball that he is unable to field.

. . . .

Hanging curve: A pitch that doesn't break and is easy to hit.

Head hunter: A pitcher with a reputation for throwing at a batter's head.

. . . .

Hidden ball trick: A play when a runner is on base and the pitcher pretends that he has the ball, but it is in fact hidden by one of the infielders, who tags the runner when he strays off the base. One of the best at it was Yankee infielder Gene Michael, who would ask the base runner to step off the bag so he could straighten it.

. . . .

High and hard: A fastball up around the letters on the batter's uniform or around the shoulders.

. . . .

Hill: The pitching mound.

. . . .

Hit it on the screws: When a batter connects solidly with a pitch.

HIDDEN BALL TRICK

Hook: Any curveball. Can also refer to a manager replacing a pitcher by giving him the hook. The term comes from a sight gag in vaudeville where a stage manager would replace a terrible performer by reaching out with a long pole with a hook on the end, similar to a shepherd's crook.

. . . .

Hoover: A good infielder who vacuums up every grounder, or a compliment about an infielder's

HOOVER

HORSEHIDE

ability to scoop up ground balls. Named after the vacuum cleaner brand, not the president.

. . . .

Horse collar: A batter who has no hits in a game. He's not feeling his oats.

. . . .

Horsehide: Though today made of cowhide, baseballs are still referred to as horsehide, as in "hitting the old horsehide."

ICE CREAM CONE

Hot corner: Third base. A **third sacker** or third baseman plays the hot corner.

. . . .

Ice cream cone: A catch made by an outfielder where most of the ball is protruding from his mitt. In this case, the batter takes a licking.

In the hole: A ball hit between the third baseman and the shortstop. Or, to a lesser extent, a ball hit in the hole between the first and the second basemen.

. . . .

Jack: To hit a homer out of the ballpark.

. . . .

Journeyman: A solid player, not a star, who is traded from team to team.

EXTRA INNINGS: Journeyman

The dependable Matt Stairs played for thirteen different teams in his nineteen seasons. Pitcher Bobo Newsom played in four decades, won twenty games three times, lost twenty games three times, and was on nine different teams. But he played for two teams twice: He was a member of three different St. Louis Browns teams and played in five different stints with the Washington Senators.

JUNKBALL PITCHER

Jug handle curve: A big curve. A **knee-buckler**. To **roll it off the table**.

. . . .

Junkball pitcher: One who throws curves, sliders, and off-speed pitches, but rarely a fastball. He nibbles at the corners and seldom throws a pitch down the middle of the plate, trying to make the batter swing at bad pitches.

KNUCKLEBALL

Keystone combination: The second baseman and the shortstop. Usually referring to a double play initiated by these two players.

. . . .

Knuckleball: A pitch thrown by gripping the ball tightly by the fingertips and throwing it in such a way that the ball usually spins only once or twice, causing it to dip and curve unpredictably. Also called a **knuckler**, a **dry spitter**, a **flutterball**, or a **butterfly**.

EXTRA INNINGS: Knuckleball

The speed of this pitch is usually only in the 60 or low 70 miles per hour range. R. A. Dickey, however, throws the pitch exclusively, and his is in the low 80s. When thrown effectively, it is a difficult pitch to hit or catch. Some catchers use oversized mitts or first baseman's gloves to snag the knuckleball. Former catcher Bob Uecker said, "The way to catch a knuckleball is to wait until it stops rolling and pick it up."

Lace it: To hit the ball hard.

. . . .

Laugher: A blowout where one team wins by a big score. Not so funny for the losers.

. . . .

Lay one down: A bunt. Usually intended to advance runners, but it can also be an attempt for a base hit. A **drag bunt** is when the batter

LAY ONE DOWN

is moving as he bunts the ball and is trying to make a single. A **sacrifice bunt** occurs when there is a runner (or runners) on base and fewer than two outs. A **squeeze bunt** is when there is a runner on third with fewer than two outs. A **suicide squeeze** occurs when the runner on third is running and the batter must make a successful bunt. A **swinging bunt** happens when the batter takes a full swing but the ball merely dribbles in front of the plate as if he had meant to bunt.

EXTRA INNINGS: Lay one down

Jackie Robinson's first Major League hit in 1947 was a bunt single; he bunted 42 times that season, collecting 19 hits.

In 1969, Pete Rose won the batting title over Roberto Clemente by bunting on his final at bat of the season.

EXTRA INNINGS: Lid lifter

In 2001, the Twins hosted the last regularly scheduled doubleheader in history, celebrating the first one, which took place on May 30, 1901. Once a common feature in baseball, doubleheaders now happen only when a makeup game is played before a regularly scheduled game.

LOOPER

Lid lifter: The first game of a doubleheader (a **twin bill**). Some doubleheaders require a separate admission for each game. Variations include afternoon and night doubleheaders, as well as morning-afternoon twin bills.

. . . .

Looper: A softly hit single.

Mendoza line: To have a low batting average. Named after a player named Mario Mendoza, who had a career batting average of .216. One theory as to how the term came about was that various Sunday newspapers would list all players' batting averages, and cutting the list off at .200 often coincided with Mendoza's name.

. . . .

Mop up: In a runaway loss, a manager looks for a pitcher to mop up and get the game over with. At least once a year, a manager will resort to using a position player to mop up a game. Hall of Fame third sacker Wade Boggs mopped up for the Yankees in a 1997 game against the Angels. He was the only pitcher in that game not to allow a run.

. . . .

Move 'em over: When runners are on first, or first and second, with fewer than two outs, a savvy batter will try to hit a grounder to the right or first-base side of the infield to advance them.

MOP UP

Murderer's Row: A lineup where every hitter is good. Usually refers to the 1927 Yankees lineup that included Babe Ruth and Lou Gehrig.

MUSTARD

Mustard: To throw a pitch harder than normal. "To put some extra mustard on it." Hold the relish and ketchup.

· · · · · · · · · · · ·

Neighborhood play: On a force play, the infielder misses touching second base because he is avoiding the runner coming from first. The umpire will usually give him the call if the fielder was ahead of the runner and made the play to avoid an injury.

NICKEL CURVE

Nickel curve: A slow-breaking curveball, often moving from 12 o'clock to 6 o'clock. A wake-up call for any batter.

EXTRA INNINGS: No-hitter

A **perfect game** is one in which the pitcher allows no hits and no runners to reach base, whether by an error, a walk, a passed ball, or striking the batter. Nolan Ryan holds the record with a whopping seven no-hitters.

A **combined no-hitter** is one in which more than one pitcher is used. A famous example of a combined no-no happened in 1918, when Babe Ruth, pitching for the Red Sox, walked the first batter in the game. He then got into an argument with the home-plate umpire and punched him in the face. The Babe was tossed from the game. Ernie Shore relieved Ruth, then retired the base runner when he tried to steal second, and proceeded to set down the next 26 batters for a combined no-hitter.

A **no-hitter superstition** holds that if a pitcher is throwing a no-hitter, no teammate, manager, or announcer is supposed to mention it for fear of jinxing him.

NO-HITTER

No-hitter: A game in which the pitcher allows no hits. A **no-no**.

. . . .

Ohfer: When a hitter has no hits in his at bats, he is said to go 0-for-3 or 0-for-4. Yankee third baseman Graig Nettles named his dog "Ohfer."

PAINT the CORNERS

On-deck hitter: The player batting next, after the one at bat. Usually, he waits in the on-deck circle. **In the hole** refers to the player hitting after the on-deck batter.

. . . .

On the interstate: A batter hitting between .100 and .200. On a scoreboard, a batting average of, say, .195 looks like I-95, the interstate highway between Boston and Miami.

PASS

Paint the corners: A pitcher who does not throw it down the middle of the plate, but rather throws it inside or outside over the edges of the plate. A Monet on the mound.

. . . .

Pass: Taking a base on balls. A walk. An **intentional pass** is when the pitcher deliberately walks a batter by throwing four pitches wide to the catcher. This might be done

EXTRA INNINGS: **Pass**

In 1924, the Major Leagues briefly outlawed the intentional walk, saying the fans resented it, and it was unfair to a good hitter. Years later, the Texas League passed a rule that a pitcher could call for an automatic walk and not have to throw four wide pitches. That didn't last either.

to set up a possible double play by putting a runner on first base, or to pass a feared slugger in a critical situation. Only five times since 1900, most recently to Josh Hamilton, has a batter been given an intentional pass with the bases loaded.

. . . .

Phantom tag: A tag by an infielder that is close to—but does not touch—the runner but is called an out by the umpire, usually a missed call.

PHANTOM TAG

EXTRA INNINGS: Phenom

In 1945, the NY Giants brought up a much ballyhooed Clint Hartung, a pitcher-outfielder considered to be a phenom, hitting .358 in the minors while winning three games on the mound. The *New York World Telegram*'s Tom Meany wrote, "Hartung's a sucker if he reports to the Giants. All he has to do is sit at home, wait till he's eligible, and he's a cinch to make the Hall of Fame."

EXTRA INNINGS: Pinch hitter

A number of hitters have extended their careers because of their ability in tough situations to come off the bench and successfully pinch hit. One of these was Dave Philley, who played for the Phillies (of course), among others. In 1958–59, he had nine straight hits, all pinch hit. He played for eighteen seasons, but half of those years he went to bat fewer than a hundred times. Lenny Harris also played eighteen years on many teams and compiled a modest .269 batting average. But he holds the record with 212 career pinch hits.

PINCH HITTER/RUNNER

Phenom (pheenom): An exceptionally talented prospect. A highly publicized rookie. Similar to a blue chipper.

. . . .

Pinch runner and **pinch hitter**: A substitute put in the game to take the place of another player.

PITCH OUT

Pitch out: A wide pitch out of the strike zone that the batter can't reach. When a catcher thinks a base runner will try to steal, he might signal for a pitch out. This allows the catcher a clear throw to second base.

. . . .

Pool cue: A batted ball hit off the top of the fat end of the bat, which bounces erratically.

EXTRA INNINGS: Pitch out

Occasionally, the pitch is not quite wide enough. When Hall of Famer Nap Lajoie stepped up to the plate in an end of the year game in 1904, the catcher thought that the runner on first base would try to steal, so he called for a pitch out. But Lajoie reached across the plate and hit it into the right field bleachers for a two-run homer. In a September 1912 game, Ty Cobb attempted the same thing and hit it for a triple, but the umpire called it a ball because Cobb had stepped out of the batter's box.

Portsider: A left-handed pitcher. Port is the left side of a ship and starboard is the right side and it is assumed that this is the origin of the term. So, why aren't right-handers called starboardsiders?

POOL CUE

PULL HITTER

Pull hitter: A batter who typically hits to the same side of the field as where he stands at the plate (a lefty hits to right field; a righty to left). A **spray hitter** hits equally well to all fields. An **opposite field hitter** hits to right field if a right-hander and left field if a left-hander. A **dead pull hitter** almost always hits to that same side, and often teams shift their fielders around to defend it.

. . . .

Punch-and-Judy hitter: A light hitter without power. A **banjo hitter**. The origin is perhaps from the puppets who hit each other, but not that hard.

RABBIT EARS

Punch out: When a pitcher strikes out a batter.

. . . .

Rabbit ears: A player who is easily upset when he hears names the other team is calling him.

. . . .

Rhubarb: An argument, usually between a player and umpire, or a manager and umpire. A rhubarb could be between several players on each team.

RIGHT DOWN BROADWAY

Ribbie: A run batted in, or RBI. If you are trying to say "RBI," it sounds like "ribbie."

. . . .

Right down Broadway: A pitch down the middle of the plate. Also known as **down Main Street** or **down the pike**.

ROSIN BAG

Round tripper: A home run. A trip around the bases. Announcer Dick Enberg's signature call on a home run was "touch 'em all." A **four-bagger, dinger, tater**.

. . . .

Rosin bag: A small mesh bag of resin or rosin (the bag was originally called a resin bag but morphed into rosin) is kept behind the pitching mound so that a pitcher can dry his fingers off. The bags were long used in dugouts, but first appeared on the field in National League spring training games in 1926. Gaylord Perry, a pitcher

RUBBER ARM

with a reputation for doctoring baseballs, would occasionally load up a ball with rosin before he threw it. The pitch would explode through a cloud of white powder, distracting the batter. The rosin bag load-up was outlawed thereafter.

. . . .

Rubber arm: A pitcher who throws many games without getting a sore arm. Mike Marshall pitched in 106 games for the Dodgers in 1974, a Major League record, and then appeared in 90 games for the Twins five years later, an American League record. Marshall, who has a doctorate in kinesiology, claims to never have had a sore arm.

. . . .

Ruthian: A long home run is sometimes called Ruthian. Other nicknames for Ruth were The Babe, The Bambino, The Sultan of Swat, The Wali of Wallop, The Rajah of Rap, The Colossus of Clout, The Maharajah of Mash, and The King of Swing. One of the first Jewish players, Mose Solomon, was nicknamed The Rabbi of Swat in homage to the Babe.

. . . .

Sawed off his bat: When a batter breaks his bat swinging at an inside pitch. Bats generally have thinner handles these days, making them more susceptible to breaking. Most bats are made of either sugar maple or ash. The maple bats, though harder, break more easily.

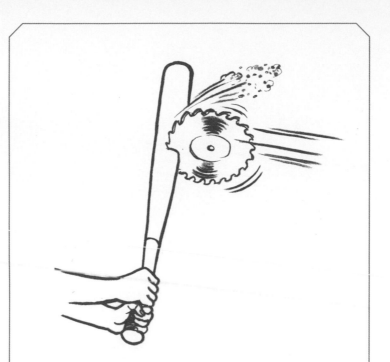

SAWED OFF

Scratch hit: Any hit that is not considered cleanly hit or fielded. In scoring, it is considered just as good as a solid single. Looks like a line drive in the box score.

SCROOGIE

Scroogie: A screwball. A pitch that curves in on a right-handed hitter from a right-handed pitcher; a natural curve from that pitcher would curve away from the hitter. Hall of Famer Christy Mathewson had a great screwball that he called a "fadeaway."

. . . .

Scrub: A bench player. Also, **scrubbini**.

Seeing-eye single: A ground ball that eludes the infielders for a hit, almost as if it had eyes and avoided the fielders.

. . . .

Seventh inning stretch: The practice of the fans standing and stretching in the middle of the seventh.

EXTRA INNINGS: **Seventh inning stretch**

A popular but probably apocryphal story is that President William Howard Taft attended a game in Pittsburgh and, sore from sitting, stood up to stretch. Upon seeing the chief executive stand, the rest of the fans, out of respect, joined the president. Whether or not that story is true, in 1910 Taft and his wife actually did surprise fans by appearing at the opening game for the Washington Senators. When one of the players asked the president to throw out the first ball, Taft obliged, starting a tradition that continues today.

SHORT PORCH

Shading a batter: If a batter hits most of his balls to one side of the field or the other, the fielders will move a couple of steps in that direction, thus shading the batter.

. . . .

Short porch: A ball field with close-in fences in the outfield, making it easier to hit a home run.

SHORT RELIEVER

Short reliever: A relief pitcher who usually throws one of the middle innings, such as the sixth, seventh, or eighth. A **closer** comes in to finish the game and protect a lead. A **long reliever**, or **middle reliever**, unlike a closer, regularly throws more than one inning.

SHOWBOAT

Showboat: A player who shows off when he hits a homer, slides in to home safely, or strikes out a batter. A **hot dog**.

EXTRA INNINGS: Showboat

Germany Schaefer, a colorful player in the first two decades of the last century, was sent in to pinch hit in a 1906 game against the White Sox. It was in the ninth, with a man on base and Schaefer's Tigers down 2–1. According to his teammate Davy Jones in *Glory of Their Times*, Germany announced to the crowd, "Ladies and Gentlemen, you are now looking at Herman Schaefer, better known as 'Herman the Great,' acknowledged by one and all to be the greatest pinch hitter in the world. I am now going to hit the ball into the left-field bleachers. Thank you." He then hit the first pitch into the bleachers for a game-winning homer. He supposedly slid into every base, announcing his progress along the way.

SIGNAL (SIGN)

Sidewinder: Another name for sidearm pitcher.

. . . .

Signal (sign): The catcher's indication to the pitcher as to what type of pitch to throw. Simple signals would be one finger for a fastball, two fingers (a **deuce**) for a curve, or three for a changeup. But on the Major League level, signals are rarely that simple. The catcher changes the signals if there is a runner on base who might steal the signs. A **coach's signal** is the sign that a third base coach gives to a batter, telling him to take a pitch or bunt or something of the sort. It could be a sign as simple as his right hand swiping across the letters on his uniform.

. . . .

Sit on a pitch: To know what the next pitch will likely be, and be ready for it. On a 3-1 count, a batter expects a fastball, a likely pitch for a pitcher to be able to throw for a strike, and will swing at one if it is over the plate. If the pitcher throws a pitch he is not expecting in that count, say a changeup, the batter may be fooled.

Small ball: A style of playing where a team moves runners from base to base with singles and stolen bases, and without home runs. In the 1980s A's manager Billy Martin's style of small ball was called "Billy Ball," as he emphasized aggressive base-running, bunting, and base stealing.

. . . .

Smoke: A fastball pitch. He throws it, doesn't blow it.

. . . .

Spitter: An illegal pitch that is thrown by wetting the fingers or wetting the ball, causing it to move erratically. The pitch, along with several others such as a Vaseline ball, was outlawed in 1920 but seventeen active spitball pitchers were allowed to continue to throw the pitch.

. . . .

Splitter: A pitch thrown like a hard **forkball** that dives down. It is thrown with a fastball motion, but comes in slightly slower than a fastball, then drops. This is accomplished by jamming the ball down between the second and third fingers.

SPITTER

EXTRA INNINGS: Spitter

Burleigh Grimes was the last legal spitballer, pitching until 1934. In 1912, when the pitch was still legal, Phillies manager Red Dooin tried to thwart Pirates spitballer Marty O'Toole by putting liniment on the ball. After licking the ball for an inning or two O'Toole's mouth was so fiery he had to leave the game.

STEALING SIGNS

Squib: A softly, not squarely, hit ball, which usually goes for an out.

Stealing signs: When a team sees what a catcher from the opposing tean is signaling to the pitcher to throw, and relays that to the batter. This can be simple, such as a runner at second base, or the base coach at first or third, stealing a sign and relaying it to the batter by yelling or standing a certain way. Or more elaborately, someone sits in the center field bleachers with a pair of binoculars, stealing the signs and relaying them in.

EXTRA INNINGS: Stealing signs

One of the most blatant sign stealing acts in history occurred in 1900 in Philadelphia when the Reds' third base coach uncovered a wire in the coaching box that led across the outfield to the Phils' locker room. There, reserve centerfielder Morgan Murphy used binoculars to steal signs and relay them to the Phils' third base coach by a buzzer hidden in the dirt. The coach would then transmit the signs to the batters.

STITCHES

Stitches: The stitching on the ball. There are 108 stitches on a baseball, which are slightly raised, creating enough resistance in the air that the pitch can curve or dip. The stitching enables a pitcher to curve a curveball or knuckle a knuckleball. A two-finger fastball is gripped *along* the seams, while a four-finger fastball is gripped *across* the seams. The two-finger fastball is one or two mph slower, and reacts a bit differently.

STRIKE ZONE

Strike zone: An imaginary rectangle that extends from the batter's knees to his armpits, and is the width of home plate. In practice, it varies from umpire to umpire and with the height of the batter. The biggest strike zone was probably that of Miami Marlins pitcher Jon Rauch, who is six-foot, eleven inches tall.

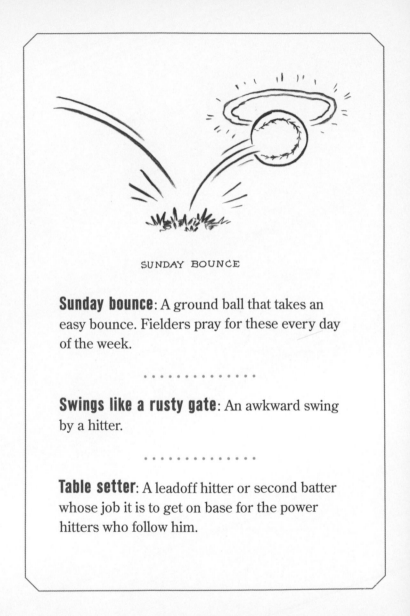

SUNDAY BOUNCE

Sunday bounce: A ground ball that takes an easy bounce. Fielders pray for these every day of the week.

. . . .

Swings like a rusty gate: An awkward swing by a hitter.

. . . .

Table setter: A leadoff hitter or second batter whose job it is to get on base for the power hitters who follow him.

TABLE SETTER

TAKING A LEAD

Taking a lead: When a runner moves off the base. A first baseman might hold the runner by standing close to the base in order to take a throw and tag him.

. . . .

Take a pitch: When a batter deliberately doesn't swing, usually on the coach's orders.

. . . .

Taking one for the team: When a batter allows himself to be hit by a pitch in order to get on base.

Telegraph a pitch: A pitcher's mannerism or grip on the ball tips off the batter or the catcher to the type of pitch that is coming.

. . . .

Texas Leaguer: A ball that loops over the infielders' heads for a hit. More often called a **flare** these days.

. . . .

30-30 club: A standard for speed and power; when a player hits at least thirty home runs and steals at least thirty bases in the same season. Thirty-eight players have accomplished this, thirteen more than once. Four of those players are in the 40-40 club: Jose Canseco, Alex Rodriguez, Barry Bonds, and Alfonso Soriano.

. . . .

Tools of ignorance: A catcher's protective equipment, consisting of a mask, chest protector, padded glove, shin guards, catcher's helmet, and cup. An ironic term, since the position calls for an intelligent player. More

TOOLS of IGNORANCE

catchers become managers than any other position. It's as if the catcher, after being hit with foul tips and flung bats and runners barreling into him, looks at himself and says, "Man, I must be an idiot to play this position."

. . . .

Triple Crown: When a batter leads a league in batting average, runs batted in, and home runs. It is a rare event, last occurring in

2 O'CLOCK HITTER

the American League in 2012 when Miguel
Cabrera accomplished it, and before that Carl
Yastrzemski in 1967. It has not happened in
the National League since 1937.

. . . .

Two o'clock hitter: A batter who hits really
well during batting practice, but not so well
during games. At one time, most games
started at three o'clock, so batting practice

was at two o'clock. There is also a five o'clock hitter, a ten o'clock hitter, etc., all referring to practice time before the start of a game.

· · · · · · · · · ·

Two seamer (or **four seamer**): A fastball.

· · · · · · · · · ·

Twin killing: A double play.

· · · · · · · · · ·

Uncle Charlie: A curveball. A **hook**. The ball breaks so sharply that it appears to drop off the table.

· · · · · · · · · ·

Up the elevator (or **silo**): A high pop-up hit straight up.

· · · · · · · · · ·

Utility player: A bench player with the ability to fill in at several positions.

UP the ELEVATOR

WASTE PITCH

Walk year: The final year of a player's contract before he becomes a free agent. A player has an added incentive to perform well in his walk year because he enhances his value as a free agent.

. . . .

Warning track power: Many of the ballparks have dirt or gravel tracks around the perimeter of the field, intended to alert an outfielder chasing a fly ball that he is approaching the wall. If a batter hits a long drive that is just short of the wall, he is said, sarcastically, to have warning track power.

. . . .

Waste pitch: A pitch that the pitcher deliberately throws outside the strike zone and is difficult to hit. It is often thrown to set up his next pitch, or to entice the batter to go after a bad pitch.

. . . .

Wheelhouse: A pitch thrown right where the batter likes it.

WHEELS & DEALS

Wheels and deals: When a pitcher winds and throws.

. . . .

White elephant: A valuable gift that you don't want and can't get rid of because it's too expensive to maintain; a nickname for the old Philadelphia Athletics, a team now located in Oakland. NY Giants manager John McGraw called the

WHITE ELEPHANT

Athletics team a bunch of white elephants, but they went on to win the 1902 pennant. They celebrated by adopting the insult as a nickname. Even today, the Athletics wear a white elephant logo on their sleeve.

. . . .

Windup: In a classic windup, the pitcher rocks his arms, lifts his non-pitching leg, and steps toward home plate to deliver the pitch. Some old-time pitchers had such an exaggerated motion that their pitching hand would touch the dirt in back of the rubber. A **stretch position** uses no windup and is used when runners are on base, to discourage base stealing.

. . . .

Work the count: Fouling off good pitches and laying off bad pitches until the batter gets to a count where he's pretty sure he can expect a fastball over the plate. Usually this is a 3-2 count, where a ball would get the batter to first.

WINDUP/NO WINDUP

WORM BURNER

Worm burner: A hard-hit ground ball. A **worm killer**. Dive for cover, worms!

. . . .

You can't walk off the island: An adage referring to Latino ball players from the Dominican Republic and Puerto Rico. In the film *Moneyball*, the free-swinging Miguel Tejada defends his relatively high strikeout rate by telling GM Billy Beane, "You can't walk your way off the island." The suggestion is that if a player wants to make an impression on scouts, he should be swinging and not trying to work the pitcher for a walk.

Acknowledgments

The authors would like to thank the terrifically talented lineup at Chronicle: Emilie Sandoz, Wynn Rankin, and Neil Egan. Cheers to the best closer anywhere, our agent Holly McGhee.

James would like to personally thank a handful of people who helped with the manuscript in some way: Marty Appel, Peter Bjarkman, Lyle Spatz, Tom Ruane, Dave Baldwin, Brian Schecter, and Mike Neill. The greatest help of course came from my wife Barbara Binswanger. And a tip of the cap to my two great collaborators, Sally and Ross.

Sally would like to personally thank Jeanne and Bob Durgan, the best fans ever. Appreciation to Bob Cook, always my ace, Ross MacDonald, who hits a dinger every time, and to James Charlton, a good battery mate.

Ross would like to personally thank the biggest cranks I know—Sally Cook and James Charlton.

About the Authors

JAMES CHARLTON is the author or editor of more than three dozen books on subjects ranging from baseball and croquet to humor and writing. He splits his time between New York City and Connecticut.

SALLY COOK is coauthor with James and Ross of *Hey Batta Batta Swing: The Wild Old Days of Baseball*. She is also the coauthor with Ray Negron of *Yankee Miracles: Life with the Boss and the Bronx Bombers*.

ROSS MACDONALD is an illustrator whose work has appeared in national and international publications including the *New Yorker*, *Newsweek*, the *New York Times*, *Rolling Stone*, and many more. He lives in Connecticut.